Juggle

Manage Your Time...
Change Your Life!

By Deanna Doss Shrodes

Juggle

Manage Your Time...
Change Your Life!

By Deanna Doss Shrodes

Entourage Publishing
2014

Juggle

www.jugglethebook.com

Entourage Publishing, Inc. 2014
www.Entourage-Publishing.com
ISBN: 978-1-942312-00-0

Endorsements

Deanna Doss Shrodes has written a practical, simplified, easy-to-read approach to time management. I love the way she shares her many personal illustrations. She is so transparent. Her approach creates the feeling that it really is possible to better manage our time. This book will encourage the reader to get started. It is a book about hope and self-leadership. It's a "make my day" kind of book. You won't want to put it down until you have read it cover to cover.
~ Dr. Bill Kuert, Assemblies of God World Missions, Kenya

* * *

This book gave me a lot of tools to help me stop dreaming about what I want to accomplish and actually DO it! For anyone who struggles with making the most of their day and needs somewhere to start, Deanna provides some very common-sense and "do-able" advice. I can't wait to start implementing this advice to manage my time better!

* * *

leader, that we weren't born to operate in "the average" but that Jehovah God created us to do exceedingly and abundantly ALL that HE has in store for our lives! Thank you for giving me the confirmation I needed right when I needed it most.

~ Torski Dobson-Arnold, CEO, Your Career Confidence, LLC, Mechanicsville, VA

* * *

This book is valuable for anyone who feels the tension of multiple obligations. Many time-management systems leave an already stressed multi-tasker feeling even more burdened than they started out! In this book, Deanna Shrodes offers practical and realistic advice and gives us permission to prioritize what is actually most important.

~ Ryan Visconti, Executive Pastor Celebration Christian Center, Mesa, AZ

* * *

Time management made simple by someone who practices what she promotes and shares practical life applications, Deanna Shrodes. A definite read if you are looking for a resource that will transform your life!

~ **Sandy Phinazee, Founder of INSPIRE Women's Conference, Jacksonville, FL**

* * *

Anyone acquainted with Deanna Doss Shrodes will instantly recognize her credibility to write a book about time management. JUGGLE is the culmination of an unending effort to make this earthly journey a "well-oiled machine." JUGGLE offers a defined road map to navigate our fast-paced culture with more ease, and less stress. Its contents offer help to men and women alike, and should be required reading for teens.

~ **Arthelene Rippy, Producer and Host of HOMEKEEPERS Television Show Christian Television Network**

Contents

Juggle

Manage Your Time...
Change Your Life!

Introduction

"How do you do it all?"
"I wish I could accomplish things like you do, but I just don't have time."
"You make it look easy."
"I wish I had your energy."

I've heard these things countless times.

Just *some* of the roles and responsibilities I carry are that of wife, mother, writer, pastor, pastor's wife, friend, certified job coach, administrator, musician, songwriter, worship leader, and conference speaker... all at the same time.

Did I mention I clean my own house too?

Most people are juggling multiple roles and responsibilities, some more than others. What are the keys to handling multiple responsibilities at the same time, with excellence?

When people used to ask me how I managed to juggle so many responsibilities and do it well, I didn't give it too much thought. I answered with things like, "It's God's grace," or "I try to be organized," or "I'm just doing the best I can."

Then one day a conference organizer called and asked if I would teach a workshop on time management. Evidently my reputation for getting things done well was more far-reaching than I realized.

I had no idea what to say.

I couldn't just get up in front of all those people and say that it was all God's grace and send them home. The task in front of me was to track what I was doing and figure out how to teach others to do the same.

I believe that an individual who learns successful time management can be compared to a church that experiences a lot of growth.

When a church explodes with growth, people ask the leadership of that church how it happened. Some pastors will say, "We don't really know how this increase came about. We just prayed, and God moved."

Sometimes people forget about the practical things they do that add up to a big difference. Perhaps they seem so basic, they appear insignificant.

While I do believe those who experience church growth prayed, I also believe their prayers were **active prayers accompanied by wise deeds.** Perhaps they didn't realize it at the time. If they reconstruct their steps, they will identify some of the contributing factors to success.

It's the same for those who are good at juggling multiple tasks to accomplish everything they want to do. While thankful for God's empowerment, there are also additional factors behind our effectiveness.

It's important to realize that nothing in your life ever changes until you change the things you do daily.

Can a person really do it all?

I've been asked this question many times.

While I don't believe any person is literally called to do it *all*, you are called to do all God has destined for you to do.

I've also come to the conclusion that we may not do it all, but we can do more than we think we can. And certainly we can do what God planned for us.

> *Daniel 11:32 says, "but the people that do know their God shall be strong, and do exploits". (KJV)*

Two of the dictionary definitions of the word "exploits" are **accomplishment** or **achievement**. So in other words, the Bible tells us that the people who know their God shall accomplish or achieve. You were

created with the potential to
accomplish and achieve great things.

The Bible gives another promise
in John 14 of what is possible in the life
of a person of faith.

> *John 14:11-13 says, "Believe me*
> *when I say that I am in the Father*
> *and the Father is in me; or at least*
> *believe on the evidence of the*
> *miracles themselves. I tell you the*
> *truth, anyone who has faith in me*
> *will do what I have been doing. He*
> *will do even greater things than*
> *these, because I am going to the*
> *Father. And I will do whatever you*
> *ask in my name, so that the Son*
> *may bring glory to the Father.*
> *(NIV)*

Greater things.
I take that to mean greater
things. Literally.

God wants to use us as an example to the world of what is possible in the life of one fully surrendered to Him, who has also put all of his or her time to good use.

I have wrestled with this issue all my life. Since I was a young girl, I have wanted to accomplish a lot. Especially in my twenties, people scolded me to slow down. They said I had my whole life ahead of me to achieve things.

The same people who were telling me to slow down and smell the roses also preached sermons about time being short and life being a vapor. The same people who said I had my whole life ahead of me preached about Jesus coming back at any moment. This was very confusing to me.

I wrestled with this message and finally decided if God says exploits are His plan for me, and instructs me to be wise in order to maximize my time, I'm going to move forward in that direction.

The truth about time

We all have the same amount of time.

Each of us gets 24 hours a day. Each hour is divided into 60 minutes, which is 3,600 seconds.

The difference is not in how much time each of us is given. The difference is what we choose to do with that time.

There was only one time that God stopped the clock for a person. God held the sun still for Joshua. Hezekiah was the individual for whom God granted this request. Many times I have prayed for a Hezekiah anointing. It has never come. I must take charge of my time.

> *"Don't ask time where it's gone. Tell it where to go." ~ John Mason*

One of my favorite scriptures is **Ephesians 5:15-17 "Be very careful, then, how you live—not as unwise but as wise, making the most of every opportunity, because the days are evil. Therefore do not be foolish, but understand what the Lord's will is." (NIV)**

So to summarize, these verses instruct us to:

- Be careful in how we live.
- Be wise in how we live.
- Make the most of every opportunity.

- Do not be foolish.
- Understand the Lord's will for us.

With this in mind, I want to ask you an important question.

What is your life really about?

Some people believe that life is about getting basic things done. This might consist of things like cooking meals, doing laundry, going to work, paying the bills, and the like.

True life is not about any of those things. Jesus talked about the Kingdom of God more than anything else in scripture.

The Kingdom of God has nothing to do with whether we keep clean socks in the drawers. Please understand, I believe being a homemaker is a worthy choice. As I mentioned before, I clean my own house and do my own laundry as well.

What I am saying is that getting chores done is not the purpose of my life or yours. Are chores a necessity of life? Yes. Are they why you were put on earth? No. God didn't put anyone on earth just to make sure there were clean socks in dresser drawers.

> *"Man's chief end is to glorify God, and to enjoy him forever."*
> *~ The Westminster Catechism*

The number one reason God created you was to have fellowship with Him. This is true of all people. God has a purpose for the gifts He has given you too.

The purpose of your life, in addition to your personal relationship with God, is to make a difference in the lives of others for eternity, starting in your home and emanating from it. So, for example, if you are a homemaker, your life is not really about socks or vacuuming, **but investing in the lives of those for whom you wash socks or vacuum.**

Now I'd like to ask you another question.

What are you aiming for?

My husband and I have pastored churches for 25 years. One thing I've realized over these many years working with people in the church is that the majority of them live aimlessly. **Most people have no game plan for their day.** They wake up and live spontaneously, figuring out what they are going to do in the moment, with no real agenda in mind. Then they wonder why there is so much confusion and lack of productivity in their lives.

Someone once said, "If you aim at nothing, that's exactly what you'll hit!"

Having an aim is important. What things are important in establishing your aim?

In the remainder of this book, I'm going to share 10 principles I've learned that make it possible for me to juggle time well to meet my aims.

Don't worry. This information is designed to free you, not overwhelm you.

This may be the most user-friendly book on time management that you've ever read! I've purposely planned it that way.

Telemarketers have called my office and tried to get me to register for 3-day conferences on Time Management. I've received direct mail campaigns that encourage me to sign up for a series of webinars that promised to save me time.

I'm convinced it's not *that* complex.

You can learn to manage your time better without sitting through a whole day or weekend of meetings. In fact, I believe you can learn to successfully juggle your weekly responsibilities and accomplish some of the greater goals you have in the 10 easy-to- understand steps I'm about to share with you.

This isn't a flash-in-the-pan theory. I've successfully juggled my daily responsibilities for 25 years reaching many bigger goals I set for myself at the same time. I use a whole lot of common sense and absolutely no rocket science. The following are my tested wisdom keys that will change your life if you just apply them.

Want-to's vs. have-to's

We all long to spend time doing what we **want** to do. I find for most people this means two things: spending time with those we love, and doing the things we are passionate about.

I've also observed that many people appear to be so overwhelmed by their have-to-do's, they seldom get to their want-to-do's. Life becomes all about "working for the weekend."

What would it be like to have **more time than just weekends** to do something you really want to do? What would it be like to actually have some time **each day** to do what you want to do?

I have a passion to help people's want-to's become reality.

Like many of you I've been at a place in my life where the have-to's seemed so overwhelming, they threatened to suffocate my want-to's.

During many seasons of my career, I've covered additional responsibilities during transitions. Through it all, I still had time for my want-to's. What, besides the grace of God, has made this possible? Following the principles of *Juggle*. Without them, my want-to's would have been impossible.

One more thing...

I wasn't born with a kind of superhuman energy that some people mistakenly believe I possess.

Actually, an important fact I want to share up front is that I live with a physical condition that affects my energy level. I could use my medical diagnosis as an excuse, but I don't.

Why am I sharing this information? To help you understand

that **this process will work for anyone!** Not only do I **not** have superhuman energy, I actually live with challenges in this regard. Even with that, the principles I am about to share have worked for me for 25 years. **They can work for you too.**

Let's get started.

Principle #1
What Tops Your List?

"If you want to make good use of your time, you've got to know what's most important and then give it all you've got."
~ Lee Iacocca

As you've probably figured out by now, I'm a Christ-follower. That means, He has top priority in my day.

It's amazing how much better my day goes when I give Him first place.

Martin Luther has been quoted as saying "I have so much to do today that I shall spend the first three hours in prayer."

I'm a different person when I don't devote private time with God daily. Not only am I downright cranky, but there's no reservoir from which to draw. My level of creativity is different. My ability to impart wisdom to others is diminished. All I have to give is me, and, quite honestly, I'm a pretty shallow person without the Lord!

Not only do I want to avoid being a bland person, I crave spending time with the Lord because I love Him. I want to reverence Him with first place in my life.

The amazing thing about doing this is the more we reverence the Lord, the more time we have, not less! The book of Proverbs tells us that reverence for the Lord actually **adds hours to our day! (Proverbs 10:27)**

Do you want more time? Then reverence God more.

I know it sounds like an oxymoron to spend more time doing something you already don't have enough time to do (like reading this book) in order to get more time to read more books, etc. But this really will pay off.

> *Matthew 6:33 says, "Seek ye first the Kingdom of God and His righteousness and all these things shall be added unto you." (KVJ)*

All. These. Things.

Let that sink in for a minute. All the dreams God placed in your heart—
everything you desire to accomplish for Him— can happen as you seek Him first and reverence Him.

For me this means discovering my best time and giving it to God first—before anything or anyone else. What is my best time? These are the finest hours of the day, the times when I am most alert and able to hear what He is saying to me through His Word and prayer.

In addition to the Bible there are many resources to use to help you draw closer to the Lord and understand what He wants you to do with your time.

It's very important that you understand what He wants you to do with your time because those are the things you will actually have the power to accomplish. God doesn't provide strength for unassigned tasks. So, it's crucial to be walking in your assignment.

Sara is a woman with a heart of gold who wants to meet every need she sees. If a friend needs help, she's the first one to step up to do something about it. When women in the church are expecting, she is the first one to volunteer to host a baby shower. The only problem is that she takes on much more than she can feasibly handle and then complains incessantly about it to those around her.

"I can't believe I agreed to do this baby shower! I'm sooooo stressed out!"... She exclaims to those who happen to be at the church while she's decorating. *"I asked someone to go by and pick up the cake from the bakery but they didn't have time, and now I'm*

trying to get all of this finished before the guests arrive. Somebody hit me in the head if I ever agree to host another baby shower again!!!"

The issue with this scenario is that Sara often takes on more than she can handle and then takes out her frustration on everyone else. Her heart is in the right place when she volunteers to do things but in the execution of those things, she becomes difficult to live with. Word sometimes gets back to the people whom she volunteered to help, and it makes them feel awkward and strains the relationship. This behavior also gives Sara's pastors pause for thought before putting her in charge of any volunteer activities because they know she will complain a lot in the process.

Perhaps you have been caught in such a cycle where your heart is in the right place when you volunteer and then you realize that you've taken on more than you can handle. Wisdom and Godly character dictates that you fulfill your current commitment without complaint. Once your current assignment is concluded, take greater care before entering an agreement to do something else.

Not completing our agreement or complaining while we do fulfill it has the potential to greatly affect our relationships and our reputations. It's important to understand our assignments, and then fulfill them to the best of our ability.

To hear from God regarding my assignment I look first to the Bible.

I recommend reading a version that is most easily understandable, like the Life Application Study Bible or the New Living Translation, which is my favorite.

Some other resources along with the Bible that really help me are:

- *Secrets of the Secret Place* by Bob Sorge (Book and Workbook)
- *Come Away My Beloved* by Frances J. Roberts
- *My Utmost for His Highest* by Oswald Chambers
- *Jesus Calling* by Sarah Young

It's so important to develop a strong private life with God separate from the time you spend at church or with others. Many Christians go to church on Sunday and then to a midweek service. Just imagine if you only ate physical food for two meals a week. I know I'd be malnourished and very cranky.

When examining the life of Jesus we see that He knew what His purpose was and He made choices that were very intentional. The results were nothing short of amazing! At the end of three years of his ministry He was able to say, **"I have brought you glory on earth by finishing the work you gave me to do." John 17:4 (NIV)**

What an amazing example!

People who don't share my faith have asked me, "How exactly does reverencing God increase my time management skills? Could you explain that to me practically?"

The simple answer to the question: "How exactly do you reverence God?" is to make spending time with Him a priority. Read the Bible, pray, meditate on the Bible, journal thoughts and prayers to God, worship by singing, or listening to songs. The more perplexing thing to understand for some who are not people of faith is the results. The supernatural really is a factor. By spending time with God, one will find their strength increased and their time maximized. Some things are better experienced than explained!

Principle #2
Find Your Purpose

"How we spend our days is, of course, how we spend our lives. There is no shortage of good days. It is good lives that are hard to come by."
~ Annie Dillard

Where are you headed? Maybe you know your direction for today, but have you looked any further down the road? What do you need to prepare for now?

Only God knows some things and He will reveal them to you in time. There are other things He will preview for you because you need to be prepared. For instance, for some things you may need to enroll in some type of training right now for something He planned for you in the future.

Just as it is helpful for organizations to have a purpose statement so it is helpful for individuals to have them.

Your purpose comes out of your passion.

To develop your purpose statement, begin to write down the things you are most passionate about.

What gets you excited?

What can't you go more than a day without thinking about?

What can't you stop talking about?

What would you always regret if you didn't do?

What would you attempt to do if you knew you could not fail?

What would you do with your time if money were no object?

At the end of your life, what is it that you want to be known for?

To identify your passion and your purpose, I've developed a worksheet you can use if you'd like a guide to assist in this process. (All worksheets referenced in JUGGLE are available for free at jugglethebook.com to download and print.)

To give you an illustration, some of my personal passions are writing, speaking, and encouraging others. In discovering my passion, I developed my purpose statement:

The purpose of my life is to encourage and empower people for God through writing, speaking and personal coaching, bringing them to a place of fulfillment and impact as they reach others with their gifts.

A purpose statement helps you to make wise decisions about where to spend your time.

Some things are not a matter of dreams and goals - they are necessities. Rare to almost non-existent is the person who has the luxury of waking up each day and exclusively doing the things they dream of doing. While I'm all for dreaming, we all have to take care of basic things in our lives that most us don't particularly enjoy— things like bill paying or taking old food out of the refrigerator and throwing it away.

However, after the necessities, or the "absolutes" as I call them, are complete, you will have time to pursue other goals, and it's very important that you choose your direction wisely. Passion and purpose are at the foundation of acting with intention.

After discovering your passion and establishing your purpose statement, you can work on listing your top areas of priority, and your short and long term goals.

Think about what you really want, not just what you're currently doing. Keep in mind if you keep doing what you're doing now, you'll more than likely keep getting the same results. Is that the outcome you want?

Resist the pressure to go in a certain direction simply because it's what others expect of you.

If you don't know exactly who you are, somebody else will not hesitate to tell you.

When my husband Larry and I were engaged, he was already youth pastor of a church while still enrolled in Bible College. I was not a part of that church as I was a counselor and choir director at a Christian home for teen girls. As our wedding day approached, I visited Larry's church several times. Soon we would be there together and I wanted to get to know the church members as much as I could. While on one of my visits, a few of the leaders met with me and said, "We're so excited for you to come! It's going to be so great to have you working with our children." The word "children" kind of caught me off guard as my husband was working with the teenagers and I wanted to clarify. I said, "Oh, you mean serving with my husband in ministering to the teenagers... right?" They said, "No, we were referring to our children's church. We really need someone to fill that role and we're counting on you to fill that position once you get here."

Evidently they already had a plan as to who their new youth pastor's wife was going to be, and what she was going to do before they knew anything about her! Needless to say, Larry saw a disaster coming and decided it would be the healthiest thing to start our marriage in a new staff situation at another church.

Throughout the years I discovered that lots of people are quite willing to tell me who they think I should be and what I should do. They will do the same for you. It's very important for us to determine our purpose and stay focused on it. Otherwise, we'll be swallowed up in someone else's expectations for us and our lives will look nothing like God intended.

> *"Give me a man who says, 'this one thing I do' and not 'these fifty things I dabble in.'"*
> ~ Dwight L. Moody

We need a God thing, not just a good thing. People call me all the time asking me to serve on this or that committee, or help out with various causes. After I take care of the necessities in my life, the time for additional things is very precious. If those things are not in line with my life's purpose and mission, I don't do them.

A big part of time management is learning to say no to the good so you can say yes to the great.

What counts most?

There is nothing greater than investing our life in the things that really matter, which actually aren't things.

People are what count.

If I don't take time each day to help somebody, what's the use of this day?

> *"If I can stop one heart from breaking, I shall not live in vain; If I can ease one life the aching, or cool one pain, or help one fainting robin up to his nest again, I shall not live in vain."*
> *~ Emily Dickinson*

Stopping to help others gives life meaning.

Some people who teach time management share how to isolate yourself from people so you can get everything done. One thing I enjoy doing is sharing with others how they can get things done so they can spend more time helping people. Because really...what could be more amazing than helping people?

Principle #3
Develop Your
Initiative List

"Don't say you don't have enough time. You have exactly the same number of hours per day that were given to Helen Keller, Pasteur, Michaelangelo, Mother Teresa, Leonardo da Vinci,

Thomas Jefferson, and Albert Einstein."
~ H. Jackson Brown, Jr.

Abraham Lincoln was reported to have said, "If I had 60 minutes to cut down a tree, I would spend 40 minutes sharpening the ax and 20 minutes cutting it down."

I spend a lot of time **preparing** to do things.

I spend more time **preparing** to do what I do than actually doing it. I think this is one of the biggest misconceptions people have about any job or role that people aspire to— the whole preparation thing. They have no idea that the majority of the work really is behind the scenes when it comes to pretty much anything.

Preparing is important because **it brings peace** while a **lack of planning leads to chaos.**

Chaos is NOT fun.

I was thinking about the word "preparation" and one of the first things that came to my mind was Preparation H. I am mindful of the fact that Preparation H commercials talk about "prompt relief." The truth about preparation, in general is that if you give proper attention to it, you'll experience true relief when deadlines arrive. If you do not give proper attention to preparation it will greatly stress you. This is true whether you're studying for a test or getting ready to speak in public. Giving attention to your readiness will truly bring **relief** in life's situations. You will have peace that you are ready for whatever comes.

The sage advice that it's better to be over-prepared than under-prepared is so true.

Time management expert Brian Tracy says that his research shows that for every minute you spend in planning you save ten minutes in execution, giving you a 1,000 percent return on energy.

Hopefully by now I've sold you on the need to PLAN. So let's do it!

The most critical week-to-week aspect of time management, aside from hearing from God about your short and long term assignment, is the development of your initiatives. These come as a result of your job description.

Yes, YOU have a job description!

No matter what your season in life you have a God-given job description. This job description exists in all phases of your life. Some people have not heeded or have ignored their job descriptions.

A stay-at-home mother has a job description. No one gets off the hook when it comes to a job description, not homemakers, or even those who are retired!

Are you listening to God when it comes to receiving your personal job description?

> *"Always remember the powerful importance of linking your habits to your life purpose."*
> ~ Mike Murdock

You are what you repeat. So what you are repeating?

I live by something I call my "Initiative List."

First, let's establish the wisdom behind a list.

Why will a list help you?

You have no doubt about what must be done.

You are able to put related tasks together or in order.

You are free from worrying about trying to remember things all the time.

You have a sense of accomplishment when you cross things off the list.

An important part of juggling all of your roles and responsibilities will be this list that you follow each week.

Each Thursday my initiative list is prepared for the coming Monday so I can see what direction I am heading in the next week.

Before I had a computer with Microsoft Outlook, everything went into a folder that I kept in my briefcase. If you are not a computer person and do things by hand writing, this will work for you just as well. Get a notebook or a folder and keep it specifically for this purpose. Now that I use a computer for everything, my agenda is on Outlook and I have it on my laptop and my phone at a glance.

To develop a master initiative list you are first going to make two lists.

List #1 contains ABSOLUTES.
List #2 contains OPTIONALS.

To decide what goes on what list:

1. **Consider what absolutely MUST be done.** These are absolutes - things you cannot live without. In other words, if you don't do these things you can't live, function, or pay your bills. Write these down under list #1 - ABSOLUTES.

2. **Consider a few optional things** that you would like to accomplish in addition to the absolutes. These are things you would really like to see happen, but can live without if they don't happen. Things like cleaning out your closet might fall into this category. Write these down under list #2 - OPTIONALS.

Once you have developed these lists, put everything under the #1 ABSOLUTES list on a new master list **in order of priority** for the week.

I personally put anything I have to do on the list whether it relates to work, home, ministry, etc. If I have to do it, it goes on the list.

How soon in the week something must be done most often indicates its priority. For instance, if I am teaching a workshop on a

Wednesday, obviously that item gets scheduled for Monday or Tuesday.

Worksheets to assist you in creating your absolutes and optionals list and your master initiative list are available at jugglethebook.com

Eat your frog first

I find I am most successful when I tackle the biggest thing I am not necessarily looking forward to doing as much first, to get it out of the way. Otherwise, I'm thinking about it too much and it affects my productivity. I like what Mark Twain once said, "If you eat a frog first thing in the morning, the rest of your day will be wonderful."

Now, before we begin to add a few things from list #2 OPTIONALS to the final list, let me explain how it's going to work...

By Saturday I compile the master initiative list all of my tasks for the upcoming week. I divide them by the number of days I'm working.

I don't always get two days off a week. Some weeks I only get one day off, other weeks I might be blessed to have two. Let's say I'm working a five day work week. And, let's say I have forty items on my initiative list that must be done that week. Then I will need to accomplish eight things a day in order to manage my time well and finish all forty things on the list by the time my days off arrive.

Eight things a day—or 40 things that week. Either way you look at it, that's the goal that needs to be met.

Through experience you will begin to see how many tasks you can reasonably handle in one week and still be healthy. If that magic number for you seems to be in the 40 range, and your "absolutes" are currently totaling 30, you know you can add no more than 10 optional things to the master initiative list that you are going to tackle in any given week.

I have accomplished anywhere from 30-100 initiatives in a week. Obviously I prefer a 30-40 initiative week! Just because you *can* get 100 things done doesn't mean you *should.*

Wisdom dictates putting the absolutes on the master list first, then filling in with as many optional items as you can and still remain healthy.

What about the leftover optional items that never get put on this week's list?

Good question.

You will not be able to get to all of the optionals in one week and that is understandable. What you are going to do is add a few optional items week by week until they all get completed.

Just to clarify the difference between an absolute and an optional:

Grocery shopping would be an absolute. Cleaning your closet would be optional.

Paying your bills would be an absolute. Reorganizing your pantry would be optional.

At the beginning of this book I shared about passion and purpose, and long and short-term goals. You may wonder how a long-term goal would be practical on a weekly initiative list. Surely you've heard that to eat an elephant, you do it one bite at a time?

At any given time I am working on larger, long-term projects. Right now I'm working on a book that is of a broader scope and will take much more time and effort. There is not a lot of free time to work on this project, and I'm surely not going to finish it in a week. I am currently allotting 15 minutes a day to this long-term goal. Some of your more challenging goals will take longer to complete and may need to be divided into small increments of time each week.

Working for 15 or 30 minutes a week on a long-term goal is better than not working on it at all. A friend of mine who is a fitness coach says that if you walk for 30 minutes you're still doing circles around everyone who's lying on the couch! Every little bit counts in moving you forward.

The key to success is following your initiative list every day. Before you give yourself permission to do anything else, tackle what is on the list.

I work as hard as I can on the list from the time I wake up, knowing the sooner I've done what's on the list for the day, the sooner I can pursue rest and recreation.

The time frame for accomplishing the initiatives is flexible within a 24-hour period. A strict daily schedule doesn't work for me in the roles I fulfill, as I serve in an area where the unexpected arises quite a bit. The good news is, I don't need to be on a regimented schedule to accomplish things under this method. **When** I accomplish the items during any given day is up to me, as long as they are done before I go to bed.

Perhaps you work a job where you have this type of flexibility. If so, you can tailor this plan to your life just as I have. If not, you can tweak it to fit your needs.

Once you establish the items that must be done each day, it's very important that you keep the goal in front of you at all times and steadily move forward to accomplish them before day's end.

It's essential to follow wisdom and not your feelings!

This brings me to my next point...

Principle #4
Why You Need to Be
Your Own Parent

"This time, like all times, is a very good one, if we but know what to do with it."
~ Ralph Waldo Emerson

The reason most people don't accomplish what they desire is

because they live with no accountability – first of all to themselves.

When we are kids we have our parents to watch over us and make sure we get things done. If we don't make our bed or do our homework, there are consequences. When we grow up and move out from under the watchful eye of our parents we might get the idea that we can do anything we want. Well, we actually *can*... but not without consequences!

Success in life takes being your own parent. It's actually something called **self-leadership**. Dee Hock, an expert on leadership, says that we need to spend at least 50% of our time leading ourselves.

How much time do you spend leading yourself?

If you can't lead yourself, how can you effectively lead anyone else?

Here's how this practically plays itself out in my life:

If I have not completed all eight items for the day and someone calls with an invitation, no matter how exciting it sounds, I say no. I play the role in my life that a Mom would play. I tell myself no when it's wise to do so.

This is so simple yet most people are not willing to do it. I've heard people say, "How fun is that?" I tell you what - not getting your work done is no fun. Being reprimanded by your boss is no fun. Being unemployed is no fun. Having ten items to do the next day versus five items is no fun either. Being under pressure at the last minute because you procrastinated is less fun than sticking to your agenda and being organized. Having nothing accomplished in life is no fun.

If you want to move forward, you can't follow your feelings all the time.

My feelings tell me to stay in bed.

My feelings tell me I'm too tired to cook or clean.

My feelings tell me to let my e-mail go unanswered for a week.

My feelings tell me I'm too tired to finish a project in the time I promised.

My feelings tell me to quit.

My feelings tell me to give up.

My feelings are terrible leaders. Now *that's* the truth!

If you are going to manage your time you have to serve notice on your feelings about who's in charge.

Feelings are real, but they don't always lead us to wise decisions. Consider making your feelings work for you. There are some positive feelings related to lists – the feeling of accomplishment, the joy of preparing for your son's birthday celebration, the excitement about delivering a fantastic presentation—leaning on those feelings will make completing tasks so much happier!

> *"No rest is worth anything except the rest that is earned."*
> *~ Jean Paul*

Leading yourself and holding yourself accountable actually frees you to do more. One of the reasons I work so hard during the week is because I want to ENJOY my day of rest and I have no problem telling people that once I've earned my rest, I take it.

What about when something pops up that you really, really, really want to do?

Has spontaneity gone out the window forever?

No. That wouldn't be healthy either.

The Bible actually says to avoid all extremes. (Ecclesiastes 7:18)

At times, a **recalculation** is needed.

When I'm riding along and take a different turn than my GPS tells me to, it recalculates the route. In a few moments time, it comes up with a way to get to the original destination albeit from a different direction.

Recalculation is something I apply to my personal weekly agenda when I am given an opportunity to do something special with my family or friends. I don't want to live so rigidly that I can't ever accept a last-minute invitation. My family members are a spontaneous bunch and it's very common for them to decide just moments before they do it that they're going to the movies, or getting ice cream, or just going out.

I am not a very spontaneous person, but I can flow with people who are. My husband often decides at the last minute that he would like us to go away overnight. Because I love my husband and want to spend time with him, I don't usually say no to these requests. However, taking advantage of an impromptu getaway requires an immediate recalculation for me.

Looking at my agenda, I see what could possibly be moved to the next day. If a change is possible, I make a decision to add a few things to the following day's agenda in order to get it all done, and on time.

The most important thing with a recalculation is that you don't put it off again. You MUST follow through after a recalculation. (This is the stuff leaders are made of, by the way.)

It's tempting after recalculation when you have ten items to accomplish the next day instead of five, or sixteen items instead of eight, to keep putting them off and avoid doing them at all. But that would lead to greater stress if you don't follow through with what you have promised to others.

A recalculation does no good if you don't actually arrive at your destination by week's end. The step where most people fail is the follow-through to actually add the deferred items to the next day's schedule.

Through careful recalculation, flexibility, and follow-through you can

get your work done and spend time
with those you love.

Principle #5
Working Your Plan

"*All glory comes from daring to begin.*"
 ~ Eugene F. Ware

All the time management tools in the world won't help you unless you actually get started.

It's not always easy to get started for an abundance of reasons.

Many people don't like to get started because starting means you might do something and fail. Other people realize the great amount of work something significant will take and they dread it.

It comes down to asking yourself: "Do I want this... or not?"

When my children were born, I had a strong desire to continue in the various leadership roles I carried. I heard everyone talk about how my life was going to completely change once I had a baby.

Although I greatly desired to have children, I feared the change a bit.

An interesting phenomenon began when I got pregnant with our oldest son. My husband and I were both staff pastors working for a senior pastor. As my pregnancy progressed, people would come up to me and hug me with a look of sadness and say, *"It's been so nice having you here, Pastor Deanna. We've appreciated our time with you."*

After several people did this, as if my vocational ministry was in the past tense, I thought, "Is something going on that I don't know about? Am I about to be fired, and everyone else knows it before I do?" I thought everything was going great. I worked hard, and the senior pastor and I were on great terms.

The truth is, the people were used to seeing women stop everything once they got pregnant or had a baby. Some thought my stepping down once I had the baby was the only right thing to do, especially for a Christian woman and a pastor's wife to boot!

A lot of people were shocked that I kept leading while I was pregnant. I found this expectation with all three of my pregnancies.

I prayed about whether it was alright to continue. When seeking God's answer, I sensed that I was not to stop. So, despite the questions I was getting from some people, I decided to keep leading. I was willing to do whatever it took to continue in ministry not only in my home but outside of it. I learned it would take a tremendous amount of planning and organization, but it was possible.

While my desire is not to pigeonhole this book into one that exclusively appeals to women, I do want to give answers many believe have been a long time coming.

Penelope Trunk, one of America's foremost career coaches

and bloggers, had this to say in a
recent blog post:

> *"Most of the time management
> advice that's out there sucks. It's
> all written by men who write
> about time management while
> their wives are at home taking
> care of their kids, or by men who
> don't have anything to do except
> write about time management.
> We need time management
> advice for people who have a real
> life."*

Real life is what I specialize in, so
today is your lucky day. I'm a woman
who has been making family, ministry,
and career work for 25 years and
counting. And right now for those of
you who are women, (or men who are
co-parenting or single dads) and want
to know my secrets of success, I'm

going to share with you the not-so-glamorous truth.

I've been a mother for 22 years now, and have served on a church staff the entire time. A week after my son was born, I began allotting two and a half hours to prepare for church. That first week set me on a course that has served me well to this day.

I learned that nothing could be left to chance. Life after having a baby mixed with full time ministry was a true juggling act.

Expecting the unexpected

Notice that in our cities, in our nation, there is an "emergency plan." The mayor, the governor, and the president all have one. So we must have one. Each day I had my plan in place.

I rarely missed work or church and was never late.

I expected the unexpected every day.

Many people struggle with getting to places on time. Some struggle with getting there at all. I have often been asked how our family has been so consistent over the years with getting five people to church services twice a week, never missing except for vacation or illness, and making it there early each time to fulfill our responsibilities.

I developed a plan for Saturdays that we've had in place for 25 years that made Sundays successful in this regard. Although I use it for Saturday, it can be used any day of the week for any purpose.

When the kids were babies, I allotted double the time it took to get ready for church. I learned that a mother must first get herself up before the children and get completely ready otherwise things are chaotic and quickly get out of control. Once I was completely ready, I began to get the kids ready.

In their infant years, I set aside two to two and a half hours. One hour for me, one hour for them, and 30 minutes for any emergency. I discovered that 30 minutes was more than enough time to change a last minute messy diaper, or completely change a set of soiled clothes. It's enough time to change a pair of hose with a runner. It's enough time to change a flat tire.

Every Saturday night I would lay the clothes out for every single family member. This meant everything down to the socks, shoes, belts, underwear, jewelry, etc.

Every Saturday night I would prepare bottles for the babies. I nursed my children but I would also freeze extra milk for emergencies. And, when they were older babies, I prepared juice for them. All of this was ready to take out of the fridge and slip in the diaper bag right before leaving for church.

Bibles, notebooks, briefcases, and diaper bags were always completely stocked, organized, and in the car the night before, except for the bottles that required refrigeration. I can't even imagine what would have taken place had I left these things to do on Sunday morning! I totally understand why many young families do not make it to church on time, or at all, if they don't prepare the night before.

The coffee pot was set the night before, and Sunday lunch prepared and in the crockpot or in the refrigerator, ready to re-heat. The table was set for lunch and breakfast plates and cups were stacked and ready on the counter. We always made sure there was gas in the car the night before. A friend used to tease me that she was surprised I didn't go so far as to put the kids in the car seats the night before!

As the years went on and the children grew, if they asked to go somewhere or do something Saturday night they knew all of this needed to be done first. If they started whining about it I would invite them to help me get it done quicker. They learned to pitch in and help in accomplishing the Saturday routine, or stop asking.

The children are all grown now, yet, as a long time habit, I still do the same things for Larry and me, and we are consistently where we need to be on time, with everything in its place.

Be aware that these principles work not only for Sunday morning church preparation, but for anytime! You can apply these principles for preparing for work the next day, or whatever other important things you have on your agenda.

Some people learned of my Saturday guidelines for our family and say that they get tired just listening to the list! The truth is, it's a lot more tiring to be running around at the last minute. It's a lot more tiring to live in chaos. It's a lot more tiring to have a bunch of things piled up because you procrastinated. It's a lot more tiring to be running late all the time or not arriving at all.

I often hear people say, "We're just in survival mode..."

God never planned that you would only survive. It's His plan for you to thrive.

Wouldn't it be nice to arrive on time all the time?

Wouldn't it be nice to always follow through on your promises to others?

Wouldn't it be nice to get rave reviews at your job every single time?

Wouldn't it be nice to never have to fear another employee evaluation again?

Wouldn't it be nice to be known as a person who always "gets it done" or "makes it happen"?

The thing is, it's TOTALLY POSSIBLE.

This can be YOU.

You don't have to just survive anymore. You can thrive.

You can get up and command the day; instead of it telling you where to go, you can take charge of it.

Principle #6
Setting Boundaries

*"Until you value yourself, you will not value your time.
Until you value your time, you will not do anything with it."*
~ M. Scott Peck

One of my favorite books is *Boundaries*, by Henry Cloud and John Townsend. The book contains great information for relationships, and can also be applied to your schedule as well.

Once you've established your passion, purpose and plan, it's important to set boundaries so that others respect your personal values.

One of the first things I learned is that it's wise to keep my calendar to myself. Others don't share my priorities; therefore, they won't always understand my decisions.

My family is my top priority next to my personal relationship with God.

A lunch date with my husband is an important appointment.

Family dinners are important.

A child's school concert is important.

My vacation time (uninterrupted) is important.

When someone asks me about a meeting and looks over my shoulder at my calendar, they may see one of these appointments and wonder why they can't be rearranged. They make value judgments about what should be important to me. Of course they do this based upon what is important to them, not what is important to me.

They may also see white space and wonder why we can't make an appointment for a certain time, not realizing that I may have a bike ride planned, or something else that is important to me in keeping wellness a priority in my life.

When someone asks me about a meeting of any kind whether professional or personal, I always say, "I'll check my calendar and get back to you." I don't ever do it in front of them, or with their input. For me this is an important part of keeping healthy boundaries.

When someone suggests something that is not workable for me, I have learned to let them know that gently.

Practice saying it with me now:

"That doesn't work for me."

Good. Now say it again, this time with more confidence.

"That doesn't work for me."

No need to be snooty. Just calmly repeat: "That doesn't work for me."

Repeat this line as often as necessary.

You'll live longer, with much more joy

Some people are confused about the definition of emergency

Back in 2001, I got a call from a woman in the church we pastored who demanded that I drop everything and advise her about her marriage problems. This isn't an unusual call for a pastor or pastor's wife to receive - we deal with these kinds of issues every day. Only this particular day happened to be my son's birthday. We were enjoying a family celebration when I received this call.

I spoke to the lady for a few minutes and then said, "Let's set up an appointment to talk tomorrow. Right now, I'm in the midst of our son's birthday celebration." She bristled at that, quite upset that I wasn't giving attention to her marital issues and told me so.

"How long have you had these marriage problems?" I asked her.

"Since 1978."

"So let me get this straight… you've had these same issues

since 1978, but it's suddenly become an emergency?"

"No, today was just the day I finally decided to call you about it..."

The fact is, **some people don't understand the true definition of emergency.**

I've had people call me and ask for someone's e-mail address, considering it an emergency.

I've received calls from people who reviewed a copy of a resume re-write who believe discussing it is urgent.

No, no, no, a thousand times no.

Re-educating about the definition of emergency is often necessary.

Heart attacks are emergencies.

Attempted suicides are emergencies.

A missing child is an emergency.

Hopefully you are getting the picture here that **very few things in life are emergencies.**

You've probably heard it said that, "A lack of planning on your part does not constitute an emergency on my part."

Learn to live by that. Don't let somebody else's lack of preparation become your emergency.

Resist the tyranny of the urgent.

Principle #7
Maximizing Every Moment

"Make use of time, let not advantage slip."
~ William Shakespeare

Use spurts of time during the week wisely

If I have even 15 minutes of free time, I use it constructively. If I am waiting for someone to arrive at my home and they are a few minutes late, I take time to clean out a small drawer in the kitchen, or I throw a load of clothes in the washing machine, or clean out a rack of the dishwasher.

Get a telephone headset, and never just talk on the phone

Always do something else while talking on the phone, unless it's a conversation that is crisis related.

One important clarification right up front: I don't multi-task on ministry crisis calls, or when I'm on a coaching call or anything that I'm compensated to do, and therefore am expected to give my 100% attention.

For many other calls besides crisis or compensated ones, I multi-task.

I have headsets for both my landline and mobile phone. I use them so much, they usually wear out about every six months! (Last Christmas Larry got me replacements for both. Yeah, you can tell your wife loves time management when she requests new headsets for Christmas.) Let me say this is one of the best investments you will EVER make! It's my number one time saver!

While I'm talking, my hands are always free and in motion, doing something else that doesn't require brain power. During a conversation I may be straightening a linen closet, throwing old things out of the fridge, or wiping down the counters.

If someone calls and says, "Hey, got a minute?" the headset goes on and I'm getting another job done while we are talking. If someone is talking for an extended length of time and I'm listening, I put it on mute as a courtesy to them, so they don't hear what I'm doing.

Catch up on podcasts

The number of podcasts I am interested in listening to is endless and rare is the occasion to just sit and listen. I subscribe to many podcasts a week by my favorite speakers. I often listen to these messages as I am cleaning the house. I also take the opportunity to listen to messages through headphones as I am working in my yard or riding my bike. It is amazing the amount of, wisdom and spiritual refreshing I receive by doing this.

Make voicemail your B-F-F

In Charles Hummel's classic, *Tyranny of the Urgent*, written in 1967, he identified the telephone as one of the worst offenders against our peace and lack of productivity. Think about it—that was before we carried our cell phones with us everywhere! Hummel is since deceased and I think he'd roll over in his grave if he could see the offenses the telephone is committing today! If telephones were affecting time management back in the sixties, consider the potential they have to completely sabotage our productivity these days.

My phone could boss me around if I let it.

I send 99% of my calls to voicemail on purpose. This enables me to screen my calls and prioritize them.

It's not uncommon for me to be in the midst of an important daily project and have three calls come in. The first call might be from one of our leaders at the church telling me they are going to miss Sunday service and need to have someone cover their responsibilities. The second call may be somebody wanting to ask my advice about a job search matter. The third call could come from a friend who has left a message asking if we can schedule lunch. In each of these cases I let the calls go to voicemail while I finish my project and get back to all three later at a time that is convenient for me. None of these issues are emergencies.

I have found most people do not let their phone go to voicemail. They take all three calls right then, and the project sits unfinished. Unfortunately, the project may not get done until the next week, month or year if they keep answering the phone in other people's time instead of their own.

Some of you need to tell the phone who's in charge! If you respond to phone calls or texts immediately while you're working on a task on your list, you will likely find that it's a struggle to get things done.

Take advantage of things designed to make life easier

Products are out there that help make time management and productivity easier. Everyone has their favorites. A few of mine in no particular order are:

- The crockpot (Love this for days that are more demanding! I usually prepare the recipe the night before, then plug in before work in the morning. Dinner is super easy.)
- Rotisserie chickens from the grocery store deli. (You can pull together a quick and nutritious dinner adding a few easy sides.)
- Clorox Wipes
- Pledge Wipes
- Windex Wipes
- Vegetables and fruits already washed and pre-cut at the grocery store

Principle #8
Taming the Communication Monster!

"Until we can manage time, we can manage nothing else."
~ Peter F. Drucker

I receive between 100-300 emails DAILY. I don't have an assistant who answers my mail. These are some

things I do to stay sane on the days
my box is closer to 300 than 100.

Delete first thing every morning

When I open my inbox each day I
delete unnecessary mail and
customarily this includes all forwards.
If I receive e-mails from lists I never
signed up to be on (and don't want to
be on), I take a moment to
unsubscribe, eliminating the need to
continue deleting that piece of mail.
Upon occasion I do get questioned by
people who say things like, "Did you
get the forward I sent you about the
supernatural frog from Mexico that
healed people as it hopped by?" and I
say, "You know, since I receive a few
hundred e-mails a day it's kind of hard
for me to keep up with ones like that."

Only touch each piece of mail once

I leave it sitting in my box throughout the day (unopened) until I am ready to answer it. If I don't have time to answer it right then I don't open it. I touch mail once, whether it's email or U.S. Mail. I don't have time to keep going back to sort through what has or hasn't been answered. So, I open it, answer it, and am done with it. The only exception to this is the rare, difficult email that might require some prayer or thoughtful response beyond the norm.

Put responses requiring more time on a to-do list, and remove them from the inbox

If a response takes more time and prayer, I try to answer the person right then saying that his or her e-mail is under consideration and I'll get back to them ASAP. Then I put the response on my to-do list so I don't forget it.

Don't carry e-mail over until the next day

I answer it all within 24 hours if possible. If it piles up from day to day it gets overwhelming and someone or something important gets overlooked.

If someone writes me a direct e-mail, requesting a response, I always answer it. If they just want me to read something to be aware of it, I don't necessarily comment on it. If they ask for a direct answer on something that's just an FYI, I might write back and simply thank them in one sentence for keeping me in the loop.

Principle #9
Self Care:
Not an Option!

"Every now and then go away,
have a little relaxation, for when
you come back to your work your
judgment will be surer. Go some
distance away because then the
work appears smaller and more of
it can be taken in at a glance and a

*lack of harmony and proportion is
more readily seen."
~ Leonardo Da Vinci*

Your health – your body (no
matter how you feel about it) does
amazing things for you each day. You
have to take care of it because it is
what houses your spirit while here on
earth and is the vehicle you use to do
everything in life. Although your spirit
is the "true you," without your body
you can't do anything practical on
earth! So it's really essential to do
things like sleep well, eat properly,
and exercise.

Rest is one of the most
important things in self-leadership.

People often ask me, "Do you
sleep?"

Yes, absolutely, because if I don't
rest, I can't think straight, or keep
going.

One of the most powerful talks I ever heard about sleep was by Arianna Huffington, co-founder and editor-in-chief of *The Huffington Post*. During this presentation, she said, *"I studied, I met with medical doctors, scientists, and I'm here to tell you that the way to a more productive, more inspired, more joyful life is: getting enough sleep."*

I agree with Huffington completely. There are a lot of recent studies and research on sleep and how it affects everything from our health to our work performance. As a Christian, I already knew how important rest was because the Bible declared it way before all of the scientific research was discussed.

God had a Sabbath day. He rested.

Jesus would come away to the mountains to rest, to pray, to get away from the crowds.

> *Mark 6:31 NIV "Then, because so many people were coming and going that they did not even have a chance to eat, he said to them, "Come with me by yourselves to a quiet place and get some rest."*

People often ask me to tell them the greatest tool I use in preparation for creating presentations, messages or songs. Without a doubt, my greatest asset is solitude.

Solitude is essential for productivity and time management.

To present the gifts that God has given me to the world, I first have to spend quiet time in cultivating them.

> *"The best gift you can give the people you lead is a healthy,*

energized, fully surrendered, focused self. And, no one else can do that for you."
~ Bill Hybels

On my day off, I don't feel guilty that I am taking time off and that I expect people not to contact me except for emergencies. I have earned my day of rest. I work hard, and I have no problem taking my sacred day for myself and my family.

Once we have ample solitude, it's important to spend some time with others as a part of restoration. Keep company with good friends who possess positive attitudes and energy. Strong relationships are a necessity for your emotional health.

Speaking of friends, don't be too proud to accept help from them when they offer it.

Everyone who achieved success in life had someone who helped them get there.

Bill Gates, CEO of Microsoft, has a photo in his office of a turtle that is up high on a fence post. It's clear that the turtle had no other way to get on that fence post other than someone putting it there. Bill has this up in his office to remind him that it takes people to get us where we need to be.

Do not be too proud to receive help, to delegate, to allow people to serve if they offer, and then thank them appropriately.

Principle #10
Just Do It!
(Don't Overthink It.)

"The bad news is time flies. The good news is you're the pilot."
~ Michael Altshuler

I've noticed that a lot of people I talk to give an enormous amount of time to **thinking about** how they will get things done. In my opinion, this is one of the greatest roadblocks to productivity.

The other day I was talking to a friend who feels the call to co-pastor, however, she hasn't actually committed to doing it yet. She doesn't know how she will "be able to do two things at once" such as raising a family while co-pastoring, and has been consumed with thinking and worrying about it. She has so much angst over it, she's stuck. I told her, "I never gave a lot of thought to whether I actually could do two or more things at once, or I probably wouldn't have ever gotten started."

While some people are still trying to figure out IF they can do something I'm usually already half way done doing it. I don't say that to brag, just to share my thought process (or lack thereof!) in fulfilling my life roles. I don't spend inordinate amounts of time wondering IF I can do it. If I determined that I'm going to do it, it's just a matter of how fast.

There have been a few times over the years that I've devoted a chunk of time worrying and analyzing "how am I going to do all this?" and it usually results in a big wad of stress that prevents me from actually delving into the work at hand. I do much better when I just leap off the edge of the cliff, and throw myself into the task. Whether I meet or exceed the goal, one thing's for sure, over-thinking would just get in the way.

Instead of thinking about whether I can do the work, I do the work. Make sense?

When you're overwhelmed

My daughter has a school friend who lives so far in the woods I can't go there without getting horribly lost every time. I even get lost when the friend is in the car with us, instructing me where to go! She lives so far back in the boondocks, my GPS loses a signal. It's maddening! So, I made a decision that my daughter is not allowed to go there anymore. The girl has to come to our house every time they want to visit in person.

I know, I know. That's probably one of the meanest things you've ever heard.

I'm being transparent here. I can't keep getting lost in the woods all the time and retain my sanity. So for the sake of my peace, I said, "She has to come to our house if you want to spend time together." I won't win

Mom of the Year for that one, but there you have it.

Although I loathe getting lost, there are times I have contemplated running away to a little cabin in the woods when things get to be too much. I let my mind drift to a little imaginary house in the middle of the woods that I run away to on purpose. Nobody can find me there.

I understand those of you who are dealing with so much you want to run away on purpose - where no one can find you.

Here are a few things that help me when I'm feeling so overwhelmed that I want to run away to my little imaginary house in the woods:

Start with something easy

Make it something small that will take you about 15 minutes to do. For me this is sometimes just cleaning off my kitchen counter. Once you see that finished space, it gives you a sense of accomplishment and a little vim and vigor to do something else. Rarely do I stop with that 15-minute project. I normally go on to do two or three other things before I call it a night.

Put on some music as a backdrop

This strategy works if you are doing menial things that don't require concentration. Go to Spotify.com or Pandora.com and make a playlist of songs that encourage you. These resources are free and I use them every day.

Make a more detailed list of things you need to do

Contrary to what you might think, going into greater detail with your list can work in your favor.

The more overwhelming things seem, it's often helpful to break your list down into smaller increments - more specific than you thought it originally needed to be. For instance, if you have two bathrooms don't just write "clean bathrooms" on the list. Make each bathroom a separate item on the list. If you have presentations to prepare don't just say, "write presentations." List each one separately. Each time you cross something off the list it's an occasion to do a happy dance.

Take breaks and treat yourself

Speaking of the happy dance, take time to celebrate and to rejuvenate. Take short breaks in between your tasks. If you've been sitting and working, get up and take a few minutes to walk around. Get a cup of coffee. I keep my favorite flavors on hand so I have something to look forward to throughout my work day.

At times when I've been running around getting tasks done, my special treat is taking 15 minutes to sit down and read a few posts by my favorite bloggers. After a brief break, I get right back to work and feel more focused.

Remember my friends, with every item crossed off the list, you are moving forward!

I began this book by telling you that we all have the same amount of time

While each of has the same amount of time, the fact that it is limited remains.

It is imperative to take control of our time and sort out the bad, the good and the great. Doing so helps us to have plenty of time to spend on the things our heart longs to do most, and spend quality time with those we love.

Take a step.

Do one thing and let it lead to another.

Then celebrate your accomplishments at every turn. I'm celebrating with you as you JUGGLE!

Acknowledgements

I'm a feedback freak. I don't know of anyone who is a great success in life without inviting honest input and taking it seriously.

JUGGLE is entirely my work with the exception of the quotations noted, yet I have not been alone while completing the work. I've heard it said that if a person has only one true friend in this life, they're blessed. Well,

I'm exceedingly blessed. I may be the richest woman in the world. I believe true wealth comes not from monetary things but from serving God, and enjoying the family and friends He has graced you with.

I approached 40 friends from different backgrounds and perspectives to help me with reviewing, editing and launching JUGGLE. I was amazed at the response from "Team 40" as I've named them.

"Anything for you!" they said.

"Of course I'll help you!" they said.

"Are you kidding? Absolutely!!" they said.

Not one of them acted as though this were an obligation. Everyone one of them told me they were honored to be a part. I am humbled at their response. They gave detailed critiques and insightful feedback. Some, out of the kindness of their hearts, reviewed the manuscript multiple times after corrections were made, to ensure an error free product.

Although I didn't mention this in the book and probably should have, the principles of JUGGLE help me keep up with all of these wonderful people in my life. :)

I want to thank everyone who helped with JUGGLE. From the bottom of my heart, I thank you for believing in me. Thank you for continually encouraging me, even when I don't ask you to. Thank you for telling me that I need to keep going. Thank you for giving validation to the messages God gives me to share. Thank you for being there for me on the days when I get the rejections that every writer gets, but naively feel like I'm the only one.

Thank you for your investment in my life.

TEAM 40:

Lisa Alexander

Larry & Debbie Ambrose

C.J. Andrews

Valerie Bell

Tina Blount

Mandy & Jeremy Caris

Joy Conley

Susanne Cox

Torski Dobson-Arnold

Sue Duffield

Jennifer Hart

Kimberly Jones

Melissa Kelly

Kathryn Kemp

Bill Kuert

Gayle Lechner

Tana Miller

Joy Andrews Morey

Bonnie Olsen

Sandy Phinazee

Christine Randall
Arthelene Rippy
Mary Ritter
Janis Russo
Debbie Shank
Tina Servello-Basinger
Larry Shrodes
Tara Sloan
Jessica Smith
Cassandra Stafford
Kelly Swift
Rich & Jennifer Tatum
Ronnelle Thomas-Brunswick
Ryan Visconti
Terri von Wood
Leanne Weber
Tammy Young

I love all of you and am blessed
to have you in my life.

~ Deanna

About the Author

Deanna Shrodes is the Women's Ministries Director for the Pen-Florida District of the Assemblies of God. She is an Assemblies of God minister and served for 27 years as co-pastor alongside her husband, Larry who is lead pastor of Celebration Church Tampa (AG). Deanna is an in-demand speaker in the United States and abroad, an accomplished musician, worship leader, songwriter and certified coach. An award winning writer, she has been featured in many publications worldwide, and is a contributing author to *Chocolate for a Woman's Courage* in the "Chocolate Series" for women, published by Simon & Schuster, *Lost Daughters: Writing Adoption from a Place of Empowerment and Peace* published by CQT Media and Publishing, *Adoption Reunion in the Social Media Age* and, *Adoption Therapy* published by Entourage Publishing, and the sole author of the books *Juggle: Manage Your Time, Change Your Life* and *Worthy to Be Found*, both published by Entourage Publishing.

She has been featured in many publications worldwide, including *The Huffington Post, Just Between Us, Woman's Touch, Enrichment Journal, Global Pastor's Wives Network, Women*

Mobilized for Ministry, and
Shepherdess Magazine.

Deanna and Larry make their home in the Tampa Bay area and have three children. Their son Dustin (24) is the youth Pastor at Celebration Church Tampa (AG). Their son Jordan (23) is a fraud recovery coordinator at Capital One, and leads the young adult ministries at CC as well as serves in music ministry. Their daughter Savanna (17) is a junior in high school and teaches a children's life group at CC, as well as participating in the dance team at her school. The family has two bulldogs, Max and Maddie.

Made in the USA
Columbia, SC
05 March 2022

57252988R00072